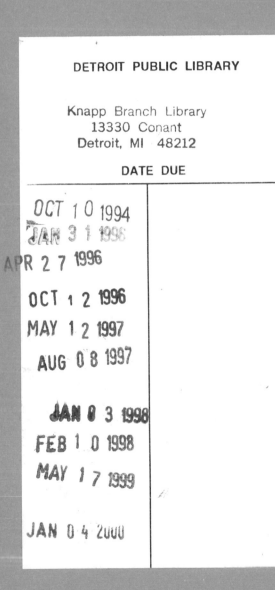

Birthday Rhymes,
Special Times

BIRTHDAY RHYMES, SPECIAL TIMES

Selected by Bobbye S. Goldstein

Pictures by Jose Aruego and Ariane Dewey

• A Doubleday Book for Young Readers • NEW YORK •

A Doubleday Book for Young Readers
Published by Delacorte Press
Bantam Doubleday Dell Publishing Group, Inc.
666 Fifth Avenue/New York, New York 10103

Doubleday and the portrayal of an anchor with a dolphin are trademarks of Bantam Doubleday Dell
Publishing Group, Inc.

Compilation copyright © 1993 by Bobbye S. Goldstein
Illustrations copyright © 1993 by Jose Aruego and Ariane Dewey

Library of Congress Cataloging in Publication Data

Birthday rhymes, special times
    selected by Bobbye S. Goldstein;
    pictures by Jose Aruego and Ariane Dewey.
        p.   cm.
    Includes index.
    Summary: A collection of poems about birthdays, by such
authors as Dr. Seuss, John Ciardi, and Jack Prelutsky.
    ISBN 0-385-30419-6
    1. Birthdays—Juvenile poetry. 2. Children's poetry,
American. [1. Birthdays—Poetry. 2. American
poetry—Collections.] I. Goldstein, Bobbye S.
II. Aruego, Jose, ill. III. Dewey, Ariane, Ill.
PS595.B57B58   1993
811'.508033—dc20   90-21488   CIP   AC

Manufactured in Hong Kong
May 1993
10 9 8 7 6 5 4 3 2 1

Acknowledgments

Grateful acknowledgment is made to the following for permission to reprint copyrighted material:

"Five Years Old" by Marie Louise Allen: From A POCKETFUL OF POEMS by Marie Louise Allen. Copyright
© 1957 by Marie Allen Howarth. Reprinted by permission of HarperCollins Publishers. / "Unwrapping" by
Yehuda Atlas: From IT'S ME by Yehuda Atlas published by Adama Books, Copyright © 1985. / "Birthdays" and

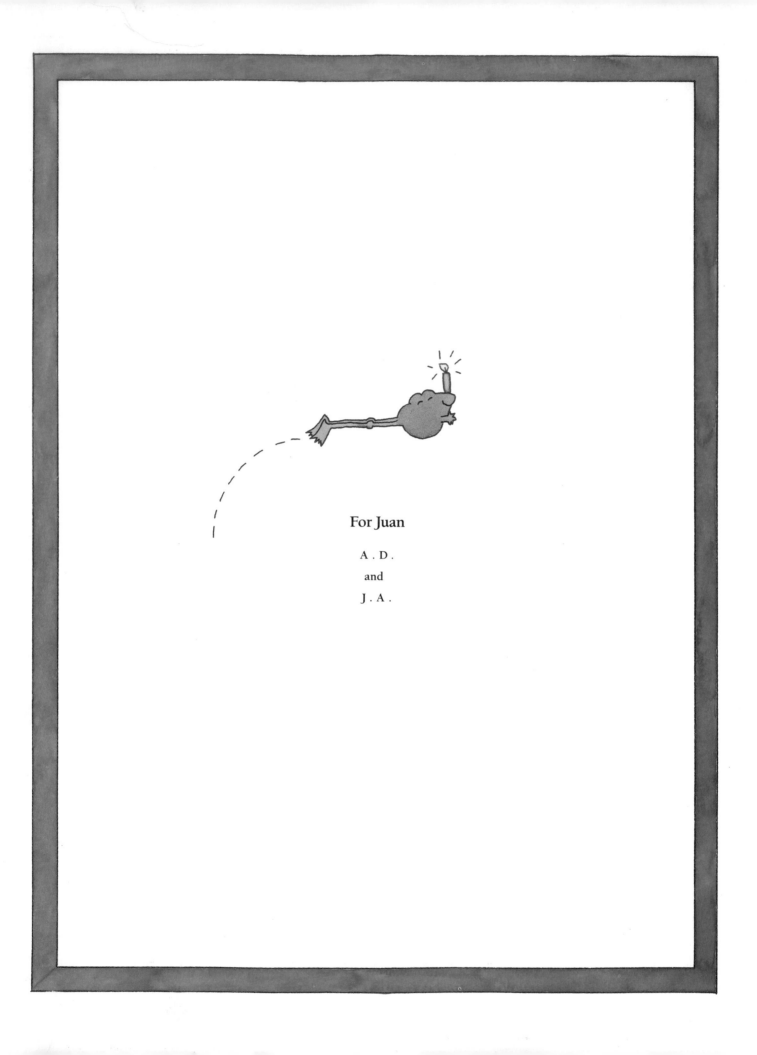

For Juan

A . D .
and
J . A .

In memory of my parents
Reverend Jacob Schwartz
and
Lottie G. Schwartz
who made birthdays and all occasions
so very special
and for
my husband Gabe and son Fred
who have continued the celebrations!

B . S . G .

CONTENTS

Special Times

Birthdays happen once a year,
And it's very nice to hear,
"Have a Happy Birthday dear!"

Bobbye S. Goldstein

Everybody Has a Birthday

Everybody has a special day,
One special day of the year.
Everybody waits and waits and waits
As that special day draws near.

Margaret Hillert

Birth Date

Aren't you glad I remembered the date?
Let's go out and celebrate!

Cecily Mopsey

13

Birthdays

Birthdays make some people glad,
Birthdays make some people sad,
Some people like a birthday surprise,
But some don't want to advertise!

Cecily Mopsey

If We Didn't Have Birthdays

If we didn't have birthdays, you wouldn't be you.
If you'd never been born, well then what would you do?
If you'd never been born, well then what would you be?
You *might* be a fish! Or a toad in a tree!
You might be a doorknob! Or three baked potatoes!
You might be a bag full of hard green tomatoes.
Or worse than all that . . . Why, you might be a WASN'T.
A Wasn't has no fun at all. No, he doesn't.
A Wasn't just isn't. He just isn't present.
But you . . . You ARE YOU! And, now isn't that pleasant.

Dr. Seuss

What Someone Said When He Was Spanked on the Day Before His Birthday

Some day
I may
Pack my bag and run away.
Some day.
I may.
—But not today.

Some night
I might
Slip away in the moonlight.
I might.
Some night.
—But not tonight.

Some night.
Some day.
I might.
I may.
—But right now I think I'll stay.

John Ciardi

THE BIRTHDAY CHILD

Everything's been different
   All the day long,
Lovely things have happened,
   Nothing has gone wrong.

Nobody has scolded me,
   Everyone has smiled.
Isn't it delicious
   To be a birthday child?

Rose Fyleman

My Birthday's in August

My birthday's in August
it's really a shame,
my party was small,
hardly anyone came.

I wish I'd been born
in November or May,
instead of a time
when my friends go away.

In August there just
isn't anyone there.
A summertime birthday
is simply not fair.

Jack Prelutsky

18

Surprises

Surprises are round
   Or long and tallish
Surprises are square
   Or flat and smallish.

Surprises are wrapped
   With paper and bow,
And hidden in closets
   Where secrets won't show.

Surprises are often
   Good things to eat;
A get-well toy or
   A birthday treat.

Surprises come
   In such interesting sizes—
I LIKE
   SURPRISES.

Jean Conder Soule

Unwrapping
my birthday gifts,
I hope I won't find
new shirts or socks
or things of that kind.

You can't expect me
to stand up and cheer
over stuff I get anyway
all through the year.

Yehuda Atlas

Choosing

Which will you have, a ball or a cake?
A cake is so nice, yes, that's what I'll take.

Which will you have, a cake or a cat?
A cat is so soft, I think I'll take that.

Which will you have, a cat or a rose?
A rose is so sweet, I'll have that, I suppose.

Which will you have, a rose or a book?
A book full of pictures?—oh, do let me look!

Which will you have, a book or a ball?
Oh, a ball! No, a book! No, a—
            There! have them all!

Eleanor Farjeon

Birthday Present

No, not something
to read, or eat,
but something
with race-away, chase-away feet.

No, not something
to ride, or wear,
but something
with rumpledy, frumpledy hair.

No, not something
inside a bag,
but something
with something outside to wag . . .

That's what I want,
the best thing yet,
and that's what I hope,
hope, hope I'll get.

Aileen Fisher

A Thought

Birthdays and Christmas
Would both be better
If no one expected
A thank-you letter.

Marchette Chute

A Birthday

Did you ever think how queer
That, every day all through the year,
Someone has a frosted cake,
And candles for a birthday's sake?

Rachel Field

Birthday Cake

The birthday cake was beautiful,
   With frosting pink and blue;
He packed it up so carefully
   And handed it to you.

You could not wait to take it home,
   You hurried from the shop;
You tried to cross the busy street,
   You stumbled, let it drop.

Policeman came and picked you up,
   A boy picked up the cake;
You took it, then called a cab,
   A cab for you to take.

The birthday cake was beautiful,
   Though mashed and crumpled some;
All the party children ate,
   Left not a single crumb!

Lois Lenski

The Ketchup Cake

Did you ever see a
Ketchup
Birthday Cake?
It's really
very easy
to make.
If you
Don't like chocolate
And you don't like candy
A ketchup cake
Would come in handy.

Just pour
Some ketchup
On plain cake.
Ketchup lovers think
It tastes
REAL GREAT!

Bobbye S. Goldstein

There was a young man so benighted,
He never knew when he was slighted.
   He went to a party,
    And ate just as hearty
As if he'd been really invited.

Author unknown

The Rose On My Cake

I went to a party,
A party for Pearly,
With presents and ice cream,
With favors and games.
I stayed very late
And I got there quite early.
I met all the guests
And I know all their names.
We sang and we jumped.
We jumped and we jostled.
We jostled and rustled
At musical chairs.
We ate up the cake
And we folded the candy in baskets
In napkins
We folded in squares.

We blew up balloons
And we danced without shoes.
We danced on the floor
And the rug and the bed.
We tripped and we trotted
In trios and twos.
And I neatly balanced myself
On my head.
Pearly just smiled
As she blew out the candles.
I gave the rose from my cake
To a friend,
Millicent Moss,
In her black patent sandals.
The trouble with parties is
All of them end.

Karla Kuskin

DOG'S DAY

They could have sung me just one song
To kind of sort of celebrate.
Or left a present on the lawn—
A juicy bone, a piece of steak—
Instead of just a candle on
This lump of dog food on my plate.
But no one cares when a dog was born,
And this ain't much of a birthday cake.

Shel Silverstein

Happy Birthday, Silly Goose!
Just today we'll let you loose
But if tomorrow you are hooked,
Then my dear, your goose is cooked.

Clyde Watson

Birthday Cake

If little mice have birthdays
(and I suppose they do)

And have a family party
(and guests invited too)

And have a cake with candles
(it would be rather small)

I bet a birthday CHEESE cake
would please them most of all.

Aileen Fisher

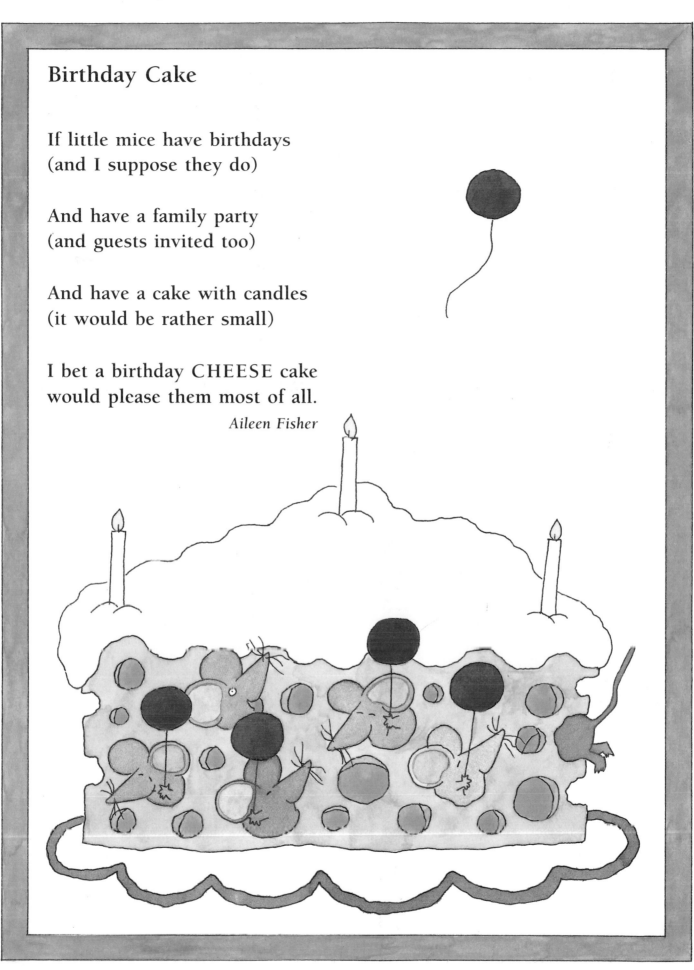

Happy Birthday, Dear Dragon

There were rumbles of strange jubilation
in a dark, subterranean lair,
for the dragon was having a birthday,
and his colleagues were gathering there.
"HOORAH!" groaned the trolls and the ogres
as they pelted each other with stones.
"HOORAH!" shrieked a sphinx and a griffin,
and the skeletons rattled their bones.

"H O O R A H !" screamed the queen of the demons.
"HOORAH!" boomed a giant. "REJOICE!"
"*Hoorah!*" piped a tiny hobgoblin
in an almost inaudible voice.
"*H O O R A H !*" cackled rapturous witches.
"Hoorahhhhhh!" hissed a basilisk too.
Then they howled in cacophonous chorus,
"*HAPPY BIRTHDAY,*
  DEAR DRAGON,
    TO YOU!"

They whistled, they squawked, they applauded,
as they gleefully brought forth the cake.
"OH, THANK YOU!"
he thundered with pleasure
in a bass that made every ear ache.
Then puffing his chest to the fullest,
and taking deliberate aim,
the dragon huffed once at the candles—
   and
the candles
all burst
   into
flame!

Jack Prelutsky

The Wish

Each birthday wish
I've ever made
Really does come true.
Each year I wish
I'll grow some more
And every year
I do!

Ann Friday

Growing Up

My birthday is coming tomorrow,
And then I'm going to be four;
And I'm getting so big that already
I can open the kitchen door;
I'm very much taller than Baby,
Though today I am still only three;
And I'm bigger than Bob-tail the puppy,
Who used to be bigger than me.

Author unknown

Cake

Four bright candles
And one to grow on,
Five bright candles
All to blow on.

I make my mouth
Round like an O.
I wait and think,
Then wish—and blow!

Miriam Clark Potter

Five Years Old

Please, everybody, look at me:
Today I'm five years old, you see!
And after this, I won't be four,
Not ever, ever, any more!
I won't be three—or two—or one,
For that was when I'd first begun.
Now I'll be five a while, and then
I'll soon be something else again!

Marie Louise Allen

Birthdays

We had waffles-with-syrup for breakfast,
   As many as we could hold;
And I had some presents extra
   Because I am nine years old.

I thanked everyone for my presents,
   And kissed 'em, and now that that's done
The family's all ready to do things,
   Whatever I think would be fun.

Marchette Chute

Dandelions

I'm picking my mother a present.
   How perfectly glad she will be
To see all the beautiful flowers
   She gets on her birthday from me.
                  Marchette Chute

My Name

I wrote my name on the sidewalk
But the rain washed it away.

I wrote my name on my hand
But the soap washed it away.

I wrote my name on the birthday card
I gave to Mother today.

And there it will stay
For Mother never throws

ANYTHING

of mine away!

Lee Bennett Hopkins

Old Man Moon

The moon is very, very old.
The reason why is clear—
he gets a birthday once a month,
instead of once a year.

Aileen Fisher

Someone Slow

I know someone who is so slow
It takes him all day and all night to go
From Sunday to Monday, and all week long
To get back to Sunday. He never goes wrong.
And he never stops. But oh, my dear,
From birthday to birthday it takes him all year!
And that's too much slow, as I know you know.
One day I tried to tell him so.
But all he would say was "tick" and "tock."

—Poor old slow GRANDFATHER CLOCK.

John Ciardi

Between Birthdays

My birthdays take so long to start.
They come along a year apart.
It's worse than waiting for a bus;
I fear I used to fret and fuss,
But now, when by impatience vexed
Between one birthday and the next,
I think of all that I have seen
That keeps on happening in between.
The songs I've heard, the things I've done,
Make my un-birthdays not so un-

Ogden Nash

Index of Authors and Titles

Index of First Lines

About the Anthologist

Bobbye S. Goldstein has compiled several collections of poetry for children, including *Bear in Mind,* illustrated by William Pène du Bois; *What's on the Menu?,* illustrated by Chris Demarest; and *Inner Chimes,* illustrated by Jane Breskin Zalben. A prominent educator, she is a former board member of the International Reading Association and the author of *Newspaper Fun: Activities for Young Children.* She is now a consultant and lecturer living in New York City.

About the Illustrators

Jose Aruego and Ariane Dewey have illustrated many books for children together, some of which they have also written. Just a few of these are *We Hide, You Seek* and *Rockabye Crocodile,* which they wrote and illustrated, and *Where Are You Going Little Mouse?* by Robert Kraus. They live in New York City.

About the Book

The illustrations for this book were drawn by Jose Aruego with pen and ink on Strathmore paper. Ariane Dewey colored them in with Winsor Newton watercolors and guache and Grumbacher watercolors. Typography is by Jane Byers Bierhorst.